HATE GROUPS

HATE GROUPS

Deborah Able

—Issues in Focus—

ENSLOW PUBLISHERS, INC.

44 Fadem Road	P.O. Box 38
Box 699	Aldershot
Springfield, N.J. 07081	Hants GU12 6BP
U.S.A.	U.K.

Library of Congress Cataloging-in-Publication Data

Able, Deborah.
    Hate groups / Deborah Able.
      p. cm. — (Issues in focus)
    Includes bibliographical references (p.) and index.
    ISBN 0-89490-627-5
    1. Racism—United States—Juvenile literature. 2. United States—Race
relations—Juvenile literature. 3. White supremacy movements—United
States—Juvenile literature. 4. Antisemitism—United States—Juvenile literature.
5. Hate—Social aspects—United States—Juvenile literature. I. Title. II. Series:
Issues in focus (Hillside, N.J.)
E184.A1A23 1995
305.8'00973—dc20   94-33429
                                                   CIP

Printed in the United States of America

10 9 8 7 6 5 4 3 2 1

Illustration Credits: Bush Presidential Materials Project, p. 80; D. K.
Welch/Southern Poverty Law Center, p. 46; Library of Congress, pp. 11,
24, 27, 30, 33, 35, 39, 67, 87; Pat Rocco/International Gay and Lesbian
Archives, p. 74; Southern Poverty Law Center, p. 57.

Cover Illustration: Pat Sullivan, AP

Contents

1

A Rising Tide of Hatred

On August 20, 1980, Joseph Paul Franklin, a thirty-nine-year-old white man in Utah killed two black men who were jogging with two white women. Later he explained his crime this way: "I'll say that it was just because they were race mixing."[1]

■ ■ ■

Between 1981 and 1987, the followers of Yahweh Ben Yahweh, the leader of the Temple of Love in Miami, Florida, were responsible for the killing of fourteen people. Yahweh taught that African Americans were the true Jews. The murderers were black; their victims were white.

■ ■ ■

On June 19, 1982, Vincent Chin, an Asian-American factory worker, stopped for a drink on his way home from work. He never reached home because two other workers beat him to death. They were both white.

■ ■ ■

On June 18, 1984, a radio talk show host, Alan Berg, stepped from his car in front of his apartment in Denver,

Colorado, his arms full of groceries. Within seconds he was dead, killed by bullets from an illegal automatic weapon wielded by members of a white supremacy group who hated Berg because he was Jewish.

■ ■ ■

On December 19, 1986, a group of black men had car trouble in the mostly white community of Howard Beach, New York. When they tried to get help, they were attacked by a group of white teenagers. As twenty-three-year-old Michael Griffith attempted to escape the violent mob, he was chased to an overpass and killed when he fell to the highway below and was hit by a car.

■ ■ ■

On November 13, 1988, three young men in Portland, Oregon, encountered three other young men. The first three were white; the other three were Ethiopian. Before their confrontation ended, Kenneth Mieske, Kyle Brewster, and Steven Strasser had murdered one of the Ethiopians, Mulageta Seraw, by beating him repeatedly on the head with a baseball bat.

■ ■ ■

On August 23, 1989, Yusuf Hawkins went to Bensonhurst, a community in Brooklyn, New York, in order to answer an advertisement for a used car. He was surrounded by a group of young men from the predominantly Italian-American neighborhood who were wielding baseball bats. Within minutes, Hawkins was mortally wounded by a gunshot. Hawkins was black; his killers were white.

■ ■ ■

On October 14, 1990, seventeen-year-old George Jones and his friend, eighteen-year-old Brian Kearchner, were bored and looking for something to do. Kearchner suggested that they "beat up a fag" for fun.[2] They went to a local adult bookstore where they encountered a man they believed was gay. They accompanied the man to his trailer, where they demanded that he give them his money. He did so, but they shot him anyway.

■ ■ ■

On August 19, 1991, Yankel Rosenbaum, a Jewish scholar who was visiting relatives in Brooklyn, was murdered by a gang of African-American men angered at the death of a black youngster killed accidentally by a car whose driver was Jewish.

■　■　■

In October 1991, George Howard, a thirty-five-year-old white man, entered a cafeteria in Killeen, Texas. He opened fire on the people eating there, killing twenty-one of them, most of whom were women. Howard was angry about Anita Hill's appearance before the Senate during the confirmation hearings on Clarence Thomas's nomination to the United States Supreme Court. Howard believed that Hill represented the growing power of women in American society, something he resented.

■　■　■

On New Year's Day, 1993, a black man, Christopher Wilson, was set on fire and burned over more than 40 percent of his body. His attackers, Mark A. Kohut and Charles P. Rourk, were white. They left a message near his body signed "KKK."

■　■　■

On July 15, 1993, FBI agents arrested eight people accused of plotting to bomb the First African Methodist Episcopal Church, assassinate Rodney King and other prominent African-American figures, and ignite a race war throughout the city of Los Angeles. All eight of the people arrested were white.

■　■　■

Different people, different years, different places, but all of these horrible incidents have one thing in common. The attackers hated the people who were their victims because in some way those people were different from them. In some cases the difference was racial, in some cases the difference was religious, in some cases the difference was sexual, and in some cases the differences were a combination of factors. But because these crimes

9

were based on people's intense dislike for other people's differences, they fall into a category that law enforcement officials call hate crimes.

Hate crimes have been increasing in the United States during the past decade or so. This is particularly ironic and disappointing because the United States, more than any other nation on earth, is made up of people of all colors, religions, and ethnic backgrounds. Our laws are designed to protect all of these people equally. The Statue of Liberty has stood in New York harbor since the 1880s to welcome strangers to a land that promises equal political and economic opportunity. Wave after wave of immigrants—from Europe, from Africa, from South America, from Asia—have come to the United States to escape the kind of racial and religious persecution that not only exists in, but is often protected by, the governments of many other countries.

Since World War II, America's commitment to civil liberties for all has grown even stronger. The civil rights movement of the 1950s and 1960s brought African Americans the rights that they were guaranteed under the United States Constitution but that had been denied them in practice. Borrowing the tactics that had worked for the civil rights movement, women, Hispanics, and homosexuals have all worked with great success for greater equality in society.

Because of this democratic tradition of tolerance for all, hate crimes appear even more horrible than other acts of violence. Not only do the attackers hurt and sometimes kill other people, they assault the very basic sense of democracy upon which our country was founded.

In the late 19th century, thousands of immigrants entered the United States through New York harbor. The Statue of Liberty, standing at the entrance to the new land, promised protection from the religious and ethnic discrimination they had faced in their homelands.

In order to combat hate crimes, it is necessary to understand the nature of these crimes and the people who commit them. Although most hate crimes are individual acts, there are many hate groups in America who condemn others because of their race or beliefs. The members of these hate groups are responsible for a relatively small number of the hate crimes. More important, however, they are responsible for spreading hatred. When a person is troubled or mentally unbalanced or lacking in self-confidence, he may listen to the words of a hate group and turn those words into violent action.

In some countries, hate groups would simply not be allowed to survive. However, a basic premise of American democracy is freedom of speech. Even when people say hurtful things with which others do not agree, their right to say them is protected by the United States Constitution. Many people who would never join a hate group and who do not believe the things that hate groups say, defend the right of hate group members to write and say what they believe. A basic reason for free speech is that if it is denied to one group, it can later be denied to other groups. Defenders of free speech believe that the best way to contradict speeches that are hateful and usually untrue is by open, truthful speech. Censorship, they believe, is not effective in fighting hate groups; rather it forces them to take their material underground where its influences among people who are susceptible to these kinds of messages are still felt.

Concerned about the rising number of hate crimes, the federal government recently passed a law requiring the Federal Bureau of Investigation (FBI) to compile statistics from local and state police about the numbers of hate crimes each year. In 1991, the first year that the law went into effect, the FBI found that in thirty-two states there had been over 4,500 hate crimes, or bias crimes as they are sometimes called because the attackers demonstrate their bias—or prejudice—against their victims. An analysis of these crimes showed that 60 percent of the assaults were based on race, 20 percent on religion, 10 percent on ethnic background and 10 percent on sexual orientation.[3]

By recording hate crimes, law enforcement officials have also been able to draw several conclusions about them. First, hate crimes tend to be extremely brutal. Because the attacker has no respect for the victim as a person of equal status in the society, he feels no remorse in destroying the person's life. Second, unlike most other crimes, hate crimes tend to be focused on strangers. In other words, the victim rarely knows his or her attacker prior to the crime. For African Americans, Jewish Americans, or homosexual Americans, who are the leading victims of hate crimes, this is very scary because it means that any stranger is a potential attacker. Third, hate crimes are often committed by people in groups. Most violent crimes, 75 percent in fact, are carried out by one person. On the other hand, over 60 percent of hate crimes are executed by more than one person, which demonstrates the importance and power of groups in the world of hate crimes.

Hate crimes are based on stereotypes—standard, oversimplified ideas—that one group of people holds about another group of people. Creating negative images about another group of people enables the hate group to justify attacking the group. For example, hate groups believe many negative stereotypes about Jews, such as that Jews control the media and the banking industry in America, that Jews are more loyal to Israel than they are to the United States, and that Jews are a greedy, aggressive group of people. Hate groups stereotype African Americans as lazy, lacking in intelligence, violent, overly sexual, and eager to live off welfare rather than to work for a living. Homosexuals are often characterized by hate groups as sexually promiscuous people who are spreading the AIDS virus throughout the world.

If a person is willing to believe that a Jewish person is a threat to the United States because of loyalty to Israel or that an African-American person is subhuman in intelligence or that homosexuals are responsible for AIDS, then it is easy to justify beating up or even murdering such a person. The members of most hate groups are white males who believe that they represent true Americans and that all these other people are anti-American. Most of these people define themselves as true Christians. However, nearly all of the organized Christian religions have denounced the actions of these people, whose violence puts them very much at odds with the peaceful and loving teachings of Jesus Christ.

Some members of hate groups can be called neo-Nazis, a term that means "new Nazis" and refers to their adherence to the philosophy and practices of Adolf Hitler, who led Germany during the 1930s and 1940s. Hitler and the original Nazis preached hatred against Jews, homosexuals, and gypsies. They killed and imprisoned millions of people before they were defeated by the United States, Great Britain, France, Russia, and the other Allied Nations during World War II.

The anger expressed by neo-Nazis and other kinds of hate groups has been triggered since the 1960s by such programs as affirmative action and social welfare programs designed to help the poorer members of American society, who are often African American, Hispanic, or immigrant. As the federal and state governments have become increasingly committed to providing equal opportunities to all Americans—especially blacks, Hispanics, and women—some of the white males who once dominated the economy feel threatened.

As different groups have received attention from the government, their public identities as separate groups have also become more noticeable. Modeling themselves on the Black Pride movement of the 1960s, different groups have chosen to separate and proclaim their differences as a way of gaining the attention necessary to assert their place in society. "Hispanic Pride," "Gay Power," and various groups within the women's movement have promoted their groups by capturing the attention of the public with their slogans, demonstrations, and organizations.

As these groups have become front-page news, they have also become the subject matter of parts of the entertainment media. Until very recently in our nation, radio, movie, and television censorship prohibited the use of even the mildest swear words on the air or on screen. Since the late 1970s, however, under the guise of freedom of speech, rock groups and moviemakers have become more and more outrageous in their use of racial and ethnic slang words of the type that are employed by the members of hate groups. These entertainers maintain that they are either joking or simply saying in song or

This sticker, found in a book at a state university library, is typical of the discriminatory sentiments expressed by hate groups. The swastika symbolizes sympathy with Hitler's campaign against Jews.

through movies what people are saying privately. People who are concerned about the amount of violence in today's entertainment world maintain that "hatred has become an integral part of American mass culture, finding expression in its art, music, politics and humor."[4]

Whether the expression of hatred in rock music is seen as freedom of expression or merely an attempt to shock and sell records, it is undeniable that there is increasing use of racial epithets and violent imagery in the lyrics of current rock music. Rappers such as Ice-T, 2 Live Crew, and N.W.A. routinely sing about violence against women and gays and justify the use of words such as "nigger" on the grounds that they are African Americans themselves. A hit song of the group N.W.A. is based on the hero blasting his girlfriend with an assault rifle. In "Watcha' Looking At?," Audio Two sings of a man who looks gay and for that reason deserves to be punched. The heavy metal group Guns N' Roses sold four million copies of their album *G N' R Lies*, which contains lyrics that most critics consider to be antiblack, antigay and anti-immigrant. In 1991, Ice Cube's album *Death Certificate* included songs that called for burning down stores owned by Koreans and for the murder of a man because he was Jewish.

Musicians are not the only entertainers who use hatred in their messages. Many comedians have made ethnic jokes, gay jokes, and jokes about women the basis of their acts. Andrew Dice Clay was able to pack Madison Square Garden for a performance in which he spewed antigay, antiblack, and antiwoman "jokes" whose stereotypes were identical to the characterizations used by hate groups in their literature. Howard Stern, one of the most popular radio announcers in the country today, daily entertains his audience and his opponents by using African Americans, Jews, Hispanics, gays, women, and the disabled as targets for his brand of humor.

In the United States, all performers are protected by the constitutional guarantee of freedom of speech. Although the Federal Communications Commission has tried at times to limit the excessive language of people like Howard Stern, these attempts have been generally unsuccessful. Most Americans support freedom of speech, and even those who are upset by the new violence in the language of mass media entertainers disagree about its impact. Many social historians maintain that music groups and entertainers merely mirror the society in which they are found. They do not create violence; they simply reflect the violence around them.

People in other nations are not so tolerant. In Germany, where the Nazis first began and where neo-Nazism today has a strong following, music groups spouting lyrics of hatred have been banned by the federal government. The band Endsieg (German for "Final Victory") sings songs about immigrants. In its hit "Kanakensong," the lyrics suggest that if a German citizen sees a foreigner, particularly a Turkish person on public transportation, the German should punch and stab the Turk. This song is based on the fear of many young native Germans that immigrant workers from Turkey are taking jobs from native workers. Under German law, anyone, including rock groups, who advocates killing other people can be tried for murder if his advice is carried out. The German constitution, adopted in 1949 when the memory of Hitler's terrible attacks on the Jews and other minority groups was fresh in German minds, prohibits inciting other people to racial hatred.

For whatever reason, violence based on hatred is on the rise in the United States and elsewhere. How to prevent its further growth and how to reduce the tensions among racial groups, between men and women, and between homosexuals and heterosexuals is a leading challenge for the American people as the twenty-first century approaches. As is the case with so much in our society, the key to solving this problem is probably education. And yet schools are increasingly the sites of hate crimes, and the perpetrators of hate crimes are most often young people, especially young men.

Learning about the groups who commit these crimes is the first step toward an educational solution to the violence they create. This book attempts to help with that first step.

2

The Roots of
Modern American Hatred

In 1967, the African-American activist H. Rap Brown, critical of Martin Luther King, Jr.'s peaceful attempts to bring about the civil rights revolution, claimed that "violence is as American as cherry pie."[1] What Brown meant was that throughout the history of the United States, from the time that the first Europeans set foot on this continent 500 years ago, people have attempted to take land or run governments by excluding other people through a variety of methods, including violence. The United States was founded on the principles of freedom, democracy, and tolerance for all. For each of these noble principles, however, there has been a dark side. The grim shadow of democracy has been the majority's domination of minorities; the shadow of freedom has been the freedom to hate and to say hurtful things about others;

and the shadow of tolerance has been prejudice against each new group that enters the society.

In 1991, two researchers, Michael and Judy Ann Newton, catalogued 8,000 acts of violence based on race or religion that had occurred in North America over the past 500 years.[2] This violence followed the same pattern as the hate crimes of the last decade: It can be defined as "harmful or destructive action against a group because of race or creed."[3]

From the beginning, the continent of North America promised new economic opportunities. For the earliest Europeans, the Vikings, this meant fresh fishing grounds. For the next wave, the Spanish, new opportunity meant gold and land, and for the dominant colonial group, the English, economic opportunity meant land and expansion of trade and businesses with the mother country. The Vikings had a history of killing those in their way; they had virtually wiped out the skrellings, the native inhabitants on Greenland, one of their first stops on the way to the New World. To the Spanish conquistadors, the Native Americans were little more than wild animals. If they resisted, they were murdered. Not only did the English continue the Spanish destruction of the native population, but as soon as they were established, they began to practice the religious and racial persecution that is at the root of modern prejudice in this country.

The first English settlers to land in North America were loyal to the king and to the Church of England. These Virginians, as they would come to be called, had little tolerance for the Puritans and Pilgrims who were settling in the area that is now Massachusetts. At home in the British Isles, the nonconformists, all who did not follow the strict doctrines of the Church of England, were the subject of persecution. With laws prohibiting their full participation in the government, they had no hope of full participation in the economic life of their native land. In large part, this is why they fled to the new continent.

It was not surprising that the Anglicans (supporters of the British monarchy and the Church of England) carried their religious prejudice with them. However, as soon as the nonconformists had established their colonies in Massachusetts Bay, Salem, Rhode Island, and other points in New England, they, too, began to practice religious intolerance. Anyone who appeared to be different was subjected to persecution that ranged from banishment into the harsh wilderness, to being burned at the stake. Burning a woman in Salem for claiming to be able to hear God's voice directly without the intervention of a Puritan minister was an example of an early hate crime. The elders of the church who pronounced her punishment were operating on exactly the same principle as the participants in modern hate crimes: By asserting her authority, the "witch" threatened their control of society.

At the same time that the northern colonists were practicing religious prejudice, their southern counterparts were introducing slavery. Beginning in 1619, the year that the first cargo of Africans was imported as slave labor for southern plantations, slavery was to create the most difficult social problem that the United States would face. By legally subjecting the enforced African immigrants to a position of perpetual bondage in the society, the early colonists created a legacy of second-class status for African Americans that is at the heart of much of today's racial hatred. From the first, slaves were forbidden to share the family integrity, education, work experience, and hope for a better future that formed the American dream for virtually all the other groups that emigrated to the New World.

By the time that the Declaration of Independence was signed in 1776, the new nation on the North American continent was well-established as a white, Protestant country. Slavery was fully entrenched in the South, and although a few people in the northern half of the nation considered slavery to be evil, very few white Americans envisioned equal political or economic status for black Americans even in the distant future.

As the colonies formed constitutions, prejudice was legalized. The federal constitution, the model for democracy in many ways, recognized slavery as an acceptable part of the new society through the "3/5 Compromise." In order to equalize the power of the northern and southern states in the newly proposed House of Representatives, the authors of the Constitution forged a compromise. Only 60 percent—or 3/5—of the slaves living in the South would count as population in determining the number of representatives a state could elect. In effect, African Americans under this plan did not count as full human beings. State constitutions written in North Carolina, Georgia, and New Jersey in 1776 forbade Roman Catholics to hold office, and the Vermont constitution, adopted the next year, stated that only Protestants could hold office.

As the new nation got underway in the early nineteenth century, religious prejudice continued to be the

Slaveowners in the American South mistreated the African Americans they held in bondage, often beating them for the slightest acts of disobedience. Even after slavery was aboiished, the idea that black Americans were second-class citizens continued.

main force behind hate crimes. The white Protestant men in power in the early 1800s appeared to have forgotten that their ancestors had once been immigrants. New waves of immigrants, eager to share in the economic boom of the new nation, faced hostility that was most frequently based on their religion. (As long as slavery was legal, there was no reason to worry about African immigrants sharing in the economic prosperity of the nation.)

Between the 1820s and the 1850s, a 'nativist' movement swept through the country. Based on the assumption that white Protestants were the only true Americans, this movement was responsible for hundreds of acts of violence, directed most often against Roman Catholics. Prior to this time, the number of Catholics in the country had been so small as to pose no threat to the ruling Protestant majority. With immigration from Roman Catholic Ireland on a sharp increase, however, the sudden surge in Roman Catholics, particularly in the cities of the Northeast, appeared to threaten the majority, even though as a total percentage of the population, Roman Catholics would never exceed 15 percent.

In the 1820s, gangs of boys in New York and Boston beat up nuns and priests in the name of the nativist movement. In 1834, the largest nuns' residence in Boston, the Ursuline Sisters' Mount Benedict Convent, was burned to the ground. That same year the inventor of the telegraph, Samuel F.B. Morse, warned in a letter to a New York paper of "A Foreign Conspiracy Against the Liberties of the United States." Morse wrote that the Pope's "henchmen" were entering the country as immigrants and planned "to establish a Romish kingdom in the Mississippi valley."[4] When the Pope sent a block of marble to be included in the construction of the Washington Monument, a gang stole it and threw it in the Potomac River.

By the 1840s, the situation had worsened. The nativist movement had become the basis for a conservative political party, the American Party. Also known as the "Know-Nothing Party" because of the secrecy practiced by their members, this group experienced a good deal of support, especially in local urban elections. The potato famine in Ireland in 1844 meant that immigration from that nation had increased. In 1845, 100,000 people emigrated from Ireland to the United States, most of them Roman Catholic. The platform of the American Party included these planks: No Catholic should hold any political office; no foreign-born Protestant should hold any political office; and people should have to wait twenty-one years before applying for United States citizenship.

The nativist movement reached its peak in the 1856 election. In the presidential race, former president Millard Fillmore ran on the American Party ticket and won one-fifth of the votes cast. The "Know-Nothings" were successful in local elections in New York, Massachusetts, Rhode Island, New Hampshire, Connecticut, Pennsylvania, Delaware, Maryland, and California. Although only 7 percent of the population in 1856 could be classified as immigrants, the popularity of the American Party demonstrated what a powerful force prejudice could be in American politics. Nearly 150 years later, David Duke would use many of the tactics of the nativists when he appealed to Louisiana voters to elect him governor and return America to "true" Americans.

The American—or "Know-Nothing"—Party gained strength in the 1840s as more and more immigrants entered the United States. Committed to a white Protestant ruling class in the United States, the Know-Nothings printed posters like this one showing their idea of an ideal American.

The nativist movement waned as the nation faced civil war. Violence and oppression had been constant factors in the lives of African Americans since their arrival on this continent. Even their arrival had been violent. Africans were captured by Englishmen and forced in chains to endure a horrible ocean voyage to the New World; any act of resistance was met by beatings and often death. Throughout the 250 years of slavery, violence against African Americans was condoned as a necessary part of keeping these people in bondage. Slave overseers were allowed to punish slaves physically— whippings were routine, and rebellious slaves were often beaten to death. Such violence against slaves properly belongs to the history of hate crimes because the only reason a person was allowed to be enslaved was the color of his or her skin. In many southern states, 1/32 of African heritage classified a person as black and thus subject to enslavement.

With the end of the Civil War, white Americans, who made up the majority of the country's citizens and who controlled the government completely, had to deal with the fact that the four million ex-slaves were now entitled by law to be citizens of the United States. Prewar southern civilization had been based on the premise that black Americans were not full citizens, that white people were superior to black people, and that the two races should never mix. Prior to the war, it had been illegal in southern states to teach slaves to read and write. Slaves were not allowed to vote, to serve on juries, to have money of their own, to own property, or even to marry legally. Slaves did not even control their own families; their white owners could sell part of a family at any time to a plantation far away where the person would never see his or her loved ones again. All of these laws and customs were intended to reinforce the idea that blacks were inferior to whites.

The fourteenth and fifteenth amendments to the Constitution gave African-American males the same political rights as white males. Although many white Americans adjusted to this change in the status of black Americans, for others the idea of sharing the political and economic life of the nation equally with freed slaves was unacceptable. They decided that the best way to prevent African-American citizens from exercising their new rights was to carry out a campaign of violence against them. This violence against African Americans has remained an ugly fact of daily life in America. From the post-Civil War lynchings in the South to the bombing of African-American churches during the civil rights movement to the burning of Christopher Wilson on New Year's Day in 1993, African Americans have faced more violent prejudice than any other group.

The idea of intimidating African Americans through violent means gave rise to one of the most infamous hate groups in American history, the Ku Klux Klan. Although the original Klan was formed by a band of ex-Confederates and operated solely in the South, the Klan expanded in the twentieth century and now operates throughout the United States. For many Americans, Klansmen, dressed in their white sheets and burning crosses on hillsides or on the front lawns of the homes of African Americans or other people Klansmen hate, typify hate groups.

The original Klan was organized in Pulaski,

To many people, the cruelest aspect of slavery was the separation of
family members in slave auctions. Husbands were sold apart from
wives, and children from their parents because black slaves were
considered to be property, not human beings.

Tennessee, by a small group of former Confederate soldiers. These young men were extremely embittered by the South's loss in the Civil War. In addition to the humiliation that all soldiers feel when they lose, these southerners felt that their whole world had been turned upside down. Virtually all of the war had been fought on southern soil, and the property damage to the South was estimated at 10 billion dollars. The emotional toll on white southerners was also great because their society was in danger of being totally rearranged. African Americans, who had been at the bottom of the social ladder, were now being given land, freedom, and the promise of education and full participation in southern politics and economic life. Not only that, they were being protected by the hated enemy, the Yankees.

In the beginning, the Klan was planned to be a fraternity of white Christian southern men who would get together for social reasons. It was not until 1867 that the idea really took hold and membership grew. In that year, an ex-Confederate general, Nathan Bedford Forrest, became the "Grand Wizard" of the Ku Klux Klan. Forrest was a superb horseman, and his nickname was the "horse wizard"; his title in the Klan derived from that nickname. Under the leadership of Forrest, the Klan was transformed into an organization of terror. These Klansmen wore sheets to hide their identities and to appear more terrifying in the night. They hoped that poorly educated, superstitious African Americans would think they were ghosts when they appeared out of the night. Their scare tactics went well beyond costumes, however. They burned homes and black schools, whipped black men who tried to vote, and lynched black men if they

31

thought they had touched—or even spoken to—white women. Wherever the Klan appeared, they burned a cross as a symbol of white supremacy.

By the early 1870s, the Klan had been so effective in terrorizing southern African Americans that almost none voted. Conservative white southerners recaptured control of southern state governments and legalized the segregation of black people. In the late 1800s, laws were passed throughout the South and in some northern states prohibiting black people from using the same public facilities as white people, from riding on the same train cars as white people, from eating in the same restaurants as white people, from serving on juries, and even from being buried in the same cemeteries as white people. Any time that an African American was even suspected of violating one of these laws, the Klan donned its sheets and went after the alleged offender. African Americans were often hanged—or lynched, as such illegal hangings were called. It has been estimated that during the years between the birth of the KKK and the end of World War I, there were more than 5,000 lynchings in the South. Often black men were hanged for appearing disrespectful to white men or for allegedly looking at white women.

By the early twentieth century, life for African-American southerners was grim. They realized that they had no future in the South where they could never fully participate in politics or in the economic system. When World War I brought the opportunity for work in the factories of the North, African Americans moved out of the South by the thousands. The Ku Klux Klan moved with them.

With the end of the First World War, the KKK

The Ku Klux Klan used scary costumes and night-time rituals to intimidate their victims. Here they are receiving candidates for membership.

boomed because they added two new groups to their targets—Jews and Roman Catholics. William Simmons, an Atlanta businessman, became the leader, or Grand Wizard, of the modern Klan. He hired two public relations experts, Edward Y. Clarke and Elizabeth Tyler, to help him recruit new members of the Klan. Seizing on Americans' disillusionment with the war, Clarke and Tyler promoted the idea that American soldiers had died because of a war that had been created by a conspiracy of international Jewish bankers and Eastern European immigrants who were either Jewish or Roman Catholic. The Klan's new motto was "100 percent Americanism." Klan leaders defined 100 percent Americanism as 100 percent Protestant and 100 percent white. To emphasize his beliefs, William Simmons liked to pull out his weapons in front of an audience, lay them on a table in front of him, and announce, "Now let the Niggers, Catholics, Jews and all others who disdain my Imperial Wizardry come on."[5] By the end of the 1920s, the modern Klan had four million members.

The Great Depression and the outbreak of World War II distracted many Americans, and Klan membership declined. During World War II, Adolf Hitler led Germany. Hitler's party, the National Socialist Party, was known by its nickname, the Nazis. Although the Nazi plans to conquer Europe were what Americans were originally aware of, they eventually learned of other Nazi plans that were so horrible that many people regard Hitler and the Nazis as the most evil people in modern history. Hitler claimed that all of Germany's problems were the fault of the Jews living in Germany and other parts of Europe. He developed a plan called "the final

William Simmons, first head of the modern Ku Klux Klan, opposed
equal rights for blacks, Jews and Roman Catholics. He gained many
followers for his "100 percent Americanism" in the 1920s.

solution" that called for the imprisonment or murder of all Jews living in Germany and in any lands that the Nazis captured. Hitler's special forces, the SS, rounded up Jews, robbing them of all their possessions and separating parents from their children. They placed them in special prisons, called concentration camps, where those who were able to work were forced to do so and those who were unfit for labor—for example, old people and children—were gassed to death. Although the Jews were Hitler's primary target, his troops treated gypsies and homosexuals the same way. When the war ended and the concentration camps were liberated by Allied soldiers, the world learned of Hitler's hatred and madness. The murder of millions of Jews has come to be called the Holocaust.

Hitler's Nazis were the most extensive hate group the world has ever known. It is because of the Nazis that hate groups today are often grouped together under the heading of neo-Nazi, a term that literally means "new Nazi." The neo-Nazis follow the teachings of Hitler and use the symbols of Nazi Germany, particularly the swastika. Not surprisingly, neo-Nazi activity began in Germany. During Hitler's peak, he was an extremely powerful leader, and German military might was feared and respected by the whole world. German neo-Nazis today seek to recapture that feeling of German supremacy and, like Hitler, blame all of their country's problems on Jews, homosexuals, and minority groups.

American neo-Nazis are white people, usually male, who believe in white supremacy and who are willing to exclude all nonwhites, non-Christians, and non-Americans through legal or illegal means from full participation in American life. They often profess to be Christians, but their words and actions have been denounced by most Christian faiths.

The horrors of the Holocaust caused many Americans to examine their own prejudice, particularly anti-Semitism. However, many Americans continued to condone prejudice against African Americans, who, in spite of making many strides toward equality during the war, were still very much second-class citizens. With prejudice came hatred and brutality.

The next wave of violence against African Americans came with the civil rights movement of the 1950s and 1960s. As black Americans gained the support of most white Americans in their quest for true equality, the minority of Americans who continued to hate African Americans on account of race became increasingly violent. On September 15, 1963, four young African-American girls were killed when their church in Birmingham, Alabama, was bombed. (A member of the Tennessee KKK, J. B. Stoner was implicated in the crime.) Civil rights workers, both black and white, were beaten, shot, and murdered throughout this period of time. Ironically, this era also brought about the greatest gains in political and economic equality for African—and other minority—Americans since the Civil War. Often this would prove to be the pattern for hate crimes. The greater the gains of the hated group, the greater the violence against them.

What happened to African Americans has also happened to other groups in the United States, especially immigrant groups. Asian Americans, whose numbers are increasing in the United States, have been victims of violence since the late nineteenth century when people from Japan and China began emigrating to the West Coast in significant numbers. After the Civil War, immigrants from China, seeking work in the mines and railroads, clustered in California. Almost from the beginning, they met a violent welcome. In 1871, a white mob burned the homes and stores of Chinese living in Los Angeles and murdered at least twenty of the Chinese in the process. In 1882, the federal government joined in the hostility against Chinese immigrants by excluding their further entry into the United States.

Although the laws against Chinese immigration were eventually rescinded, violence against Asian Americans continued. During the early twentieth century, the Japanese were the targets of hatred and violence. Anti-Japanese feelings culminated in the imprisonment during World War II of thousands of Japanese Americans in concentration camps on the West Coast. Most of the people who were imprisoned were American citizens; many of them had been born in the United States. Solely on the basis of their ethnic identity, they were accused of being threats to the United States while we were at war with their ancestral country. It should be noted that we were also at war with Germany and Italy, but German Americans and Italian Americans were not forced to give up their homes nor were they imprisoned as were the Japanese.

Since World War II, many other Asian Americans have been faced with violence and discrimination. In 1989, Jim Loo, a Chinese American living in North Carolina, was murdered by two white men who erroneously believed that he was Vietnamese and who blamed

At the beginning of World War II, the United States government ordered all Japanese Americans living on the West Coast to be rounded up and placed in concentration camps. These people lost their property and their jobs solely because of their ethnic identity.

him for the deaths of American soldiers in the Vietnam War. American soldiers during the Vietnam War routinely used racial epithets to describe both their South Vietnamese allies and their North Vietnamese enemies. They carried this prejudice home with them when they were discharged. Vietnam veterans or not, many Americans believed the advertising campaign recently undertaken by the Detroit automobile industry that blamed the Japanese car makers for slow business and unemployment among American car workers. This kind of thinking led to the murder of Vincent Chin described in Chapter 1. It is also the kind of thinking that led Patrick Purdy to open fire with an automatic weapon on a schoolyard in a predominantly Asian neighborhood in Stockton, California, killing five children and wounding thirty others. Purdy explained his crime by saying, "The damn Hindus and boat people own everything."[6]

Thus modern-day immigrants from Asia have joined the ranks of Americans who have been victims of hate crimes. From the Irish and Eastern-European Jews of the nineteenth century to the Asians and Hispanics of the twentieth century, immigrants to America have found not only the welcoming beacon of the Statue of Liberty but also violence from hate groups and individuals who share the hostility of those groups. During the past two decades, another group of people, not immigrants, has joined the roster of those whose lives and property are endangered by hate groups.

Since the 1970s, homosexual Americans have become more and more visible in our society. As has been true for other groups in the United States, the more visible and more tolerated they have become, the more susceptible to hatred and violence they have been. In 1969, the New York City police raided the Stonewall Inn, a bar in Greenwich Village that catered to gay customers. Prior to this raid, gays had greeted such raids passively. On this night, however, they fought back. "Stonewall" became a symbol of gay pride and gay activism for greater acceptance and greater civil rights. The AIDS epidemic of the 1980s galvanized gay rights activists even more because a high percentage of the victims of this disease were gay men. Conversely, attacks against gays increased because hate groups publicized the belief that gay men were responsible for the spread of AIDS throughout the population. The National Gay and Lesbian Task Force, a gay activist organization, began compiling statistics on violence against gay men and lesbians. Between 1988 and 1991, they found that acts of violence against gays increased 161 percent in the cities of Boston, Chicago, New York, Minneapolis/St. Paul, and San Francisco, cities where the gay population is highly visible. In 1991 alone, more than a dozen people were killed simply because they were—or were suspected of being—gay.[7]

The inclusion of gays on the list of targets for hate groups has clearly accelerated the violence against them. Gays have joined African Americans, Jews, and Asian Americans as victims of hate-group rhetoric and action. In the past, many gay Americans were able to avoid detection because, unlike African Americans and Jews, they were able to keep their identity as homosexuals secret. As gays "come out of the closet"—that is, openly express their homosexuality—they are more prone to attack by those who hate them.

41

3

Hate Groups

Although most hate crimes are not committed by people who belong to organized hate groups, organized hate groups are extremely important in understanding the hate crimes that are committed. Because these groups are well organized, they are able to influence a great number of people. Hate groups hold meetings to recruit new members and to publicize their feelings.

Hate groups often have newsletters to communicate with their members. During the last decade, they have become increasingly sophisticated about using modern technology to communicate. Hate groups use computer networks, public access television stations, and even video games to get their message across to their supporters. These methods are very effective. Many observers who follow the activities of hate groups estimate that the number of people who formally belong to hate groups probably represents only 10 percent of the total number of people who read the literature published by the groups and share their beliefs.

No one knows when an unaffiliated person or group of people commits a hate crime whether or not they may have been influenced by pamphlets or a television program written by or sponsored by an organized hate group. Understanding the philosophy and programs of the major hate groups in the United States is a good way to begin to understand the thinking of all people who commit hate crimes.

The Ku Klux Klan (KKK)

The oldest and best-known hate group in America is the Ku Klux Klan. For over 125 years, the Ku Klux Klan has remained true to its white supremacist roots in the states of the Civil War Confederacy. It has continued the use of strange names and the practice of secret rituals that began with Nathan Bedford Forrest. Today each new member of the Klan is given a booklet that explains the philosophy and rules of the Klan so that new members will understand the traditions of the group they are joining. This booklet is called the Kloran, a mix of the words Klan and Koran (the religious book of rules used by the Islamic religion). Each local area is organized as a den with a "Cyclops" as its leader. The Cyclops is assisted by twelve Terrors and two Nighthawks. Local dens are organized as Provinces and the Provinces are joined together as Realms. The Realms are headed by Grand Dragons, and the whole organization is under the control of the Grand Wizard.

Although the names sound silly, the KKK is anything but silly. One woman, who has left the Klan and regrets ever having joined, recalled that at weekly meetings of her den, she helped teach the "lesson of the day."[1] One such lesson involved a situation in which an African-American child had been injured in a car accident. The Klan members gathered for the "lesson" were asked whether they would use mouth-to-mouth resuscitation to save the child's life. The correct answer, which they had to shout in unison, was "no." At parades and weekend gatherings, Klansmen and Klanswomen demonstrate against Jews, blacks, Asians, homosexuals, and Hispanics. A typical antigay banner carried at many Klan rallies reads, "Thank God for AIDS."

By the 1980s, there were three major Klan leaders and three major branches of the organization. In spite of its growing membership (estimated at 10,000 at its peak in the mid-1980s), many people thought that the Ku Klux Klan no longer existed. However, the emergence of David Duke as a national political figure convinced most Americans that the Klan—or at least Klan thinking—is still a powerful force. Duke had been the Grand Wizard of the Klan from the mid-1970s until 1980. By the middle of the 1980s, he had renounced his Klan membership, calling it a "youthful mistake."[2] However, he ran for the Louisiana state legislature in 1989 on a platform that sounded ominously like the white supremacy of the KKK. He also founded an organization entitled the National Association for the Advancement of White People in the early 1980s.

In a newsletter produced for his new organization in 1983, Duke explained the views that have remained at the heart of his political campaigns. They mirror the philosophy of the KKK. He wrote:

> Immigration along with non-white births will make white people a minority totally vulnerable to the political, social, and economic will of blacks, Mexicans, Puerto Ricans, and Orientals. A social upheaval is now beginning to occur that will be the funeral dirge of the America we love. I shudder to contemplate the future under nonwhite occupation; rapes, murders, robberies multiplied a hundred fold, illiteracy such as in Haiti, medicine such as in Mexico, and tyranny such as in Togoland.[3]

Duke won the election for state legislator. Then in 1990 he decided to use the same platform that had won him a seat in the legislature to make a bid for the governorship of Louisiana. What Duke told the Louisiana voters was that the white citizens of Louisiana and of the United States in general had lost their political and economic power because of affirmative action and government spending on such programs as aid for teenage mothers and other forms of welfare payments. Duke implied that the people who benefited from government handouts were always African Americans, Hispanic, or immigrants.

Many of the voters of Louisiana were persuaded by what he had to say—but not enough to make him governor. Although he was officially a registered Republican, his ideas were simply a more refined version of his earlier Klan thinking. By maintaining that the problems in American society were the responsibility of nonwhites, he was still preaching hatred. Even more devastating to

Although many Americans like to think that the Ku Klux Klan is part of the country's past, the modern Klan is very active in some areas of the nation.

many observers was Duke's ability to bring racism into American politics as a legitimate platform.

An important aspect of Klan membership is belief in Christianity. Although the vast majority of American Christians stress love and tolerance for all as basic tenets of their religion, hate group Christians use their religion to exclude others, not include them. The followers of the most extreme example of this kind of Christianity are called Identity Christians.

Identity Christians

Although Identity Christians do not have a central church organization as do Baptists or Presbyterians or Methodists, for example, they share a common ideology among themselves. The Anti-Defamation League (A.D.L.), a Jewish civil rights organization, has called their beliefs the glue that binds together the different hate groups operating in America today. The A.D.L. is particularly wary of Identity Christians because strong anti-Semitic feelings are at the heart of their preaching. Identity churches have sprung up all over the United States since the movement was founded in 1946 by Wesley Swift, a Grand Wizard of the KKK. Identity Christians believe that the "chosen people" referred to in the Christian Bible are not the Jews, which is what most other Christians believe. Instead, they believe that God's chosen people were the white Europeans and Englishmen who settled North America. They also believe that all nonwhites and Jews are descendants of Cain, Adam and Eve's evil son. They believe that Jews are children of

Satan who conspire at all times to overthrow the white Christians.

Identity Christians rewrite history with Jews as the villains. A typical Identity pamphlet, written by David Lane, one of the men convicted of conspiring to kill radio host Alan Berg, included this interpretation of American history:

> At the time the Jews took over our monetary system via the Federal Reserve, and instituted the income tax in 1913, the White race constituted about 40 percent of the Earth's population. Since then, the Jews have instigated two World Wars and fomented the Russian Revolution. These three events alone resulted in the death of over 80 million white Christians, most of them being young males and the genetic cream of our race.
>
> Next they laid such heavy taxes on the White workers of the world that it became, if not impossible, very financially impractical to have children. At the same time, the Jews took the taxes from the labor of productive Whites and gave it to non-Whites, both here and abroad, encouraging them to have from 10-20 children. They used their media to insult and emasculate the White man while depicting non-White males to be heroes so White women would desert their race by the millions.
>
> The result is that the percentage of child-bearing women in the world today who are White and married to White men is at best four percent.[4]

There are perhaps fifty different Identity congregations scattered throughout the United States. Among them are the Mountain Church of Jesus Christ the Savior in Cohactah, Michigan. Another Identity church is the New Christian Crusade Church whose pastor, James

K. Warner, has called the anniversary of the Statue of Liberty "Mud Flood Day." (Among Identity Christians, a common name for immigrants, African Americans, and Hispanics is "mud people.") Other churches include the Ministry of Christ Church in Mariposa, California, and the Lord's Covenant Church in Phoenix, Arizona.

The most famous—or infamous—of the Identity churches, however, is Richard Butler's Church of Jesus Christ Christian in Hayden Lake, Idaho. In an interview with a *Newsweek* reporter, Butler explained his beliefs:

> When the Declaration of Independence talks about 'one people,' it's not talking about a nation made for Asia, Africa, India [or] the Soviet Union. That's a document based on a Christian people. We have watched like frightened sheep as do-gooders sniveling about the underprivileged gleefully grabbed our children by the nape of the neck and rubbed their faces in filth to create equality.[5]

What is most disturbing about Butler's church is that it gave rise to a military group that converted the Identity message into a campaign of terrorism in the mid-1980s.

The Order

During the early to mid-1980s, a vicious group of men launched a terrorist attack on the United States. Originally either members of the Ku Klux Klan or followers of Identity churches or the neo-Nazi National Alliance, they were led by Robert Mathews, a zealot who would die in 1984 in a shoot-out with federal authorities. His organization was called the Order.

The Order was described by one FBI agent as a "small cadre of individuals dedicated to violence [and] engaged in para-military activities."[6] Although small in number, they were described by the director of the Federal Bureau of Investigation, William Webster, as "more dangerous than the Klan groups from which they emanated."[7]

In 1984, FBI agents searched the home of Gary Lee Yarbrough in Sandpoint, Idaho. They were looking for Yarbrough's brother. Yarbrough, however, shot at the agents, intensifying their interest in his house. When they gained entry, they found a shrine to Hitler and the gun that had been used to kill Alan Berg, the outspoken liberal radio commentator from Denver, Colorado. Berg also happened to be Jewish.

In the course of the investigation, the FBI unraveled the history of the Order, which was also called the White American Bastion or the Silent Brotherhood. For at least three years, this group, under the direction of Mathews, had robbed and murdered in preparation for the creation of a "neo-Nazi homeland."[8] Taking his lead from Butler's preachings in Hayden Lake, Mathews added to the extreme theology the writings of neo-Nazi William Pierce, author of *The Turner Diaries* and leader of the National Alliance.

In this novel, which became Mathews' blueprint for a right-wing revolution, a race war is financed by a small guerrilla band through robberies and assassinations. The reason for the race war is the takeover of the world by a Jewish international conspiracy under whose tyranny whites are forced to intermarry with blacks and Asians and government loans are given to mixed couples who live in white neighborhoods. A group of white super-patriots under the leadership of the hero, Turner, overthrows the Jewish government, destroys Israel with nuclear weapons, and creates a white Christian paradise.

To Mathews and his followers in the Order, *The Turner Diaries* were not fiction. They repeatedly referred to the government of the United States as ZOG, the Zionist Occupational Government, a reflection of their belief that Jews (also sometimes called Zionists because of their support of the state of Israel) had taken over America. They planned to overthrow ZOG, but before doing that, they needed money for arms and ammunition and they planned to assassinate a few key figures, among them Henry Kissinger, Norman Lear (a television producer)—and Alan Berg.

Between 1983 and 1984, the Order managed to steal almost $4 million dollars, most of it at gunpoint. Before each robbery, members of the group would join hands around one of their babies, who represented the future of the Aryan race, as they called white Christians, and would chant, "From this time on I have no fear of death. I know that I have a secret duty to deliver our people from the Jew, the mud people and all who would dilute the Aryan race. One God, one race, one nation."[9]

After Berg's murder, members of the Order hid out throughout the Northwest, successfully evading law enforcement officials. One by one, however, they surrendered and were tried and imprisoned. The last hold-out was their leader, Mathews, who refused to give himself up. In the end, he was trapped on Whidby Island outside Seattle, Washington. After a gunfight with federal agents, the house where he was hiding caught on fire, and he perished in the blaze.

Mathews' last letter revealed the depth of his commitment to white supremacy. He wrote:

> The stronger my love for my people grew, the deeper became my hatred for those who would destroy my race, my heritage. . . . By the time my son had arrived, I realized that White America, indeed my entire race, was headed for oblivion unless white men rose and turned the tide. The more I came to love my son, the more I realized that unless things changed radically, by the time he was my age, he would be a stranger in his own land, a blond-haired, blue-eyed Aryan in a country populated mainly by Mexicans, mulattoes, blacks and Asians.[10]

Although the Order's spree of violence ended with Mathews' death, he has become a martyr to Identity Christians. His picture hangs next to Hitler's picture in Richard Butler's church in Idaho. The church can only be reached by traveling along a private driveway guarded by armed men with swastikas on their uniforms. A sign at the end of the driveway proclaims that "Whites Only" are welcome to enter. Butler holds an annual memorial service for Robert Mathews, and new young men are being recruited to carry on the battle.

The Posse Comitatus

At the same time that Robert Mathews and the members of the Order were waging war against ZOG, another group of Americans was also doing battle with the federal government for similar reasons. The Posse

Comitatus, founded in 1969 by Henry Lamont Beach, may well be one of the largest of the formal right-wing hate groups operating in the country today.

Posse comitatus is Latin for "power of the county." Members of this group refuse to accept any authority higher than the county sheriff. Like the members of the Order, they believe that the federal government is in the hands of a Jewish conspiracy. Throughout the 1970s, the Posse Comitatus operated in small groups. Its very nature as an organization that fought central control meant that the various groups worked independently. One of the most violent of the local posses was led by Gordon Kahl, who became a Posse Comitatus legend. Kahl, a failed farmer, blamed his financial problems on income taxes and social security payments foisted on American farmers by the evil forces that had taken over the government. He wrote, "These enemies of Christ have taken their Jewish Communist Manifesto and incorporated it into the Statutory Laws of our country and thrown our Constitution and our Christian Common Law (which is nothing other than the Laws of God as set forth in the Scriptures) into the garbage can."[11]

In 1983, two federal marshals in North Dakota attempted to arrest Kahl for income tax evasion. He killed them. A decorated World War II veteran, Kahl holed up in a farmhouse in Smithville, Arkansas, and held off an impressive array of lawmen, killing the local sheriff and wounding several others before he himself was killed. Like Mathews, Kahl became a martyr to the cause for other hate-group members. The image of the lone warrior holding off scores of federal agents single-handedly reinforced the mission of those people who believe that their cause is not only just but divine.

In spite of Kahl's death, the Posse Comitatus thrived. During the 1980s, the Internal Revenue Service, the federal organization responsible for collecting taxes, had to add a whole new unit to deal with nonpayment of taxes by increasing numbers of Americans who espoused the Posse Comitatus view that income taxes were part of the Jewish conspiracy to ruin the American way of life. In Wisconsin, James Wickstrom ran for state office on a platform supported by the Posse Comitatus. He advocated tax revolt and violence. Wickstrom's political career failed, and he ended up in prison. However, for a short time, he and his hate-group philosophy provided a springboard for the introduction of racism into American politics.

Skinheads

The Posse Comitatus, the Order, and the Ku Klux Klan are upsetting to most Americans when they hear about them. Most of the time, however, they are invisible. Far more terrifying to many people because of their increasing visibility in American cities are the violent, white-supremacist youths who join skinhead gangs. Skinheads not only act scary, they look scary. Their extreme haircuts, military garb, and combat boots reinforce their violent image. They often wear the number 88 as shorthand for "Heil Hitler" because h is the eighth letter of the alphabet.

The association with Hitler reinforces the neo-Nazism practiced by most skinheads. Skinheads began in Europe, first in England and then in Germany. Recent estimates of the number of skinhead youths in Germany run as high as 30,000 out of a population of 78 million. Although German law is far more repressive in dealing with hate-group activity than is American law, skinhead youths have a flourishing underground culture. Skinheads listen to Oi! music, which advocates violence against nonwhites and Jews, and play video games such as "Aryan Test," where the object is to earn points by killing Jews, and "Concentration Camp Manager," where the winner is the person who kills the greatest number of Turks.

There are conflicting reports about the numbers of skinheads in the United States, but the perception is that their ranks are increasing. In 1989, skinheads marched in the annual KKK parade in Pulaski, Tennessee, demonstrating their solidarity with older white supremacy groups. Skinheads tend to organize in small local groups and are found in areas as different as New York City and small towns in Utah. Bands of skinheads have colorful, expressive names such as the American Frontists, Confederate Hammerskins, the Doc Marten Stompers, and the White Workers Union.

When the FBI thwarted the plan to start a race war in Los Angeles in the summer of 1993, they found that members of the group called the Fourth Reich Skinheads were in the forefront of the plot. The Fourth Reich Skinheads were only two years old as a hate group, but in their court appearance on the charges of attempting to bomb the A.M.E. church and assassinate Cecil Murray, the African-American pastor of the church, members of the group admitted to other bombings, including a synagogue and the home of a African-American family.

In 1993, the Anti-Defamation League published a report on the growing menace of skinhead groups. According to their survey, there were 1,500 skinheads in 12 states in 1988, and five years later there were 3,500 skinheads in 40 states. The A.D.L. credits various skinhead groups with the murder of more than twenty people since 1990.

White Aryan Resistance (W.A.R.)

Among the skinheads' victims was a young Ethiopian man, Mulageta Seraw. On November 13, 1988, he was walking with two companions on a street in Portland, Oregon. Three members of a skinhead group, East Side White Pride, attacked Seraw, beating him with a baseball bat and stomping him with their boots until they had crushed his head and killed him. Kenneth Mieske, Steven Strasser, and Kyle Brewster were found guilty, and Mieske is serving a life term in jail. At his trial he explained that he killed Seraw because he was black; after four years in prison, he still expressed no regrets about his actions.[12]

When he heard about the Seraw murder, Morris Dees, a famous civil rights lawyer and the founder of the Southern Poverty Law Center, felt that the members of East Side White Pride had not acted alone. The Southern Poverty Law Center joined with the Anti-Defamation League to prosecute Seraw's murderers. Dees acted as chief counsel. He believed that the young men had been recruited to kill by an older, more

Morris Dees has worked with many people, including the citizens of
Mobile, Alabama, in an effort to redress the impact of hate crimes.

well-established hate group. He accused Tom Metzger, founder and head of White Aryan Resistance, of sending agents from W.A.R. to Portland to stir up the skinheads. Dees brought a civil case against Metzger on behalf of the Seraw family.

For two years investigators from the Southern Poverty Law Center worked at establishing a connection between W.A.R. and East Side White Pride. The A.D.L. discovered that Dave Mazzella, an agent of the White Aryan Resistance, had indeed been sent to Portland to recruit young white men to be soldiers in the hate war that Tom Metzger, and his son John, and their followers were advocating. Arguing that the Metzgers and their organization were responsible for inciting the skinhead youths in the murder of Mulageta Seraw, Dees brought a wrongful death suit on behalf of the Seraw family against Tom Metzger and his son, John, and against the organization itself. The jury agreed with Dees. Tom Metzger was forced to pay $5 million in damages and John $1 million, and W.A.R. was fined $3 million. In an angry response to the judgment, Tom Metzger used the kind of language that revealed that the jury and Dees were right in their estimate of his goals. He said, "We will put blood on the streets like you've never seen and advocate more violence than both world wars put together."[13]

Estimates of how many Americans support Tom Metzger and W.A.R. range from fewer than 20,000 to more than 100,000. Certainly W.A.R. is one of the largest, most successful hate groups in the West. Although he is based in California, Metzger reaches a large number of people throughout the country via his television program "Race and Reason," which is telecast in at least fifty markets on public access television. And television is not the only technology that Metzger uses to communicate with supporters and to recruit new members. W.A.R. also has a computer bulletin board that Metzger uses to broadcast his message of white supremacy.

Metzger pretends to be an ardent champion of free speech. Like many people who are anti-Semitic, he believes that Jews control the mass media in the United States, including film, television, and radio. For that reason, he welcomes new technology such as public access television and computer networks that are not so easily controlled. Under a 1964 federal law, public access television channels must provide free time slots to anyone who wants them on a first-come, first-served basis without censorship. In 1993 that law was modified to prohibit "obscene materials, sexually explicit conduct or material promoting or soliciting unlawful conduct."[14]

Although several groups have tried without success to shut down Metzger's program on the basis that it advocates violence, "Race and Reason" has remained on the air. Metzger argues that he is simply stating an opinion. He points to other programs with opposing views that are just as violence laden. For example, there is a program in New York City hosted by an African-American man named Ta-Har. On a recent show, Ta-Har, who claims to be a leader of the Black Israelites, claimed, "We're going to be beating the hell out of you white people. . . . We're going to take your little children and dash them against the stones. . . . We're going to rape and ravish your white women."

Metzger claims that Ta-Har's statements reinforce what W.A.R. preaches about African-American men. He uses Ta-Har's program to justify his own violent, antiblack statements. On a typical broadcast of "Race and Reason," Metzger begins, "Hi, this is Tom Metzger . . . blazing a trail of real free speech, free speech for white working people for a change. 'Race and Reason' is an island of free speech in a sea of managed and controlled news."[15] By grabbing onto the issue of free speech, Metzger is able to justify his racist, anti-Semitic rhetoric as a legitimate expression of ideas.

Metzger has not always been head of W.A.R. He began his political life as a member of the John Birch Society, an anticommunist organization that flourished in the 1950s and 1960s. He supported the segregationist politics of Alabama's governor George Wallace in the 1960s and by the 1970s was a campaigner for David Duke and served as Grand Dragon of the California Realm of the Ku Klux Klan when Duke was the Grand Wizard. After campaigning for David Duke in Louisiana, Metzger ran for office in California. Although he has not won any major election, he has a strong following around San Diego, and he has attracted as many as 75,000 votes in state-wide elections.

W.A.R. is somewhat different from other hate groups. As Metzger explains it, "W.A.R. wears no uniform, carries no card, and takes no secret oaths; [it] doesn't require you to dress up and march around on a muddy street; [it] works the modern way, with thousands of friends doing their part on the job, behind the scenes, serving their race."[16]

In spite of the judgment against W.A.R. in the Seraw case, Metzger and his organization are going strong. When the Fourth Reich Skinhead plot to start a race war in Los Angeles was uncovered, W.A.R. was implicated. Among the eight people initially arrested by the FBI, several were affiliated with W.A.R. Metzger, however, denied that he had known anything about the plot. Whether he was part of this particular plan or not, it is clear from his show and his writings that W.A.R., under the direction of Tom Metzger, is a hard-line hate group.

In addition to the groups profiled here, there are countless other small groups, many with a central connecting agenda—the establishment of white Christians as the superior group of people in America. Among these smaller groups are the Covenant, the Sword and the Arm of the Lord (C.S.A.), a para-military organization that rebuilt the weapon used to kill Alan Berg; the California White Resistance movement; the Aryan Brotherhood, which is active in prisons throughout the country; the SS Action Group, which patterns itself after Hitler's storm troopers; the National Alliance; the American Nazi Party; the Universal Order; the National Socialist League; and many others that espouse anti-semitism and white supremacy.

In a campaign speech in 1992, Bill Clinton spoke out against "the voices of intolerance . . . that proclaim that some families aren't real families and some Americans aren't real Americans."[17] He could have been describing the members of hate groups.

4

Why People Hate

Why do some people hate so much? What is there in the personalities of the members of hate groups that makes them hate people who are different from them? Why are they willing to commit violence—or at least condone it in others?

These questions have puzzled law enforcement officers, social workers, prison officials, clergy, and government officials. In fact, everyone who comes in contact with people who hate or commit hate crimes tries to figure out what motivates the haters. Unfortunately, there are no easy answers to these questions. If there were, hate crimes could possibly be stopped. In the meantime, analysts try to look at the people who have committed hate crimes to see if there are any patterns in their lives.

Three of the most obvious similarities among hate

group members are their age, their sex, and their race. Most of the members of hate groups are white males under thirty.[1] Most of the people who commit violent crimes and are not formally associated with any organized hate group are also white males under thirty.[2] The criminals currently serving time for the murder of Michael Griffith in Howard Beach, the murderers of Yusuf Hawkins in Bensonhurst, Vincent Chin's assailants in Detroit, the killers who conspired to murder Alan Berg in Denver, the attackers who beat Julio Rivera to death in New York, the arsonists who burned Christopher Wilson in Miami, the plotters who await trial for their alleged plan to start a race war in Los Angeles—for the most part, these people were young, white, and male.

In his analysis of these haters, Morris Dees has called them "violent, angry and deeply troubled" and has concluded that "they generally come from deeply troubled, dysfunctional families and are fundamentally damaged long before they swing their first baseball bat at someone or plant their first pipe bomb."[3] Many of the young haters obviously do fit Dees' and other sociologists' descriptions. For example, Greg Withrow, who, along with John Metzger, helped found the White Student Union on a number of college campuses around the United States, grew up in a house where he was verbally and physically abused by a violent, racist father. By the age of thirteen, he was homeless and living on the streets.

Another hater who had a troubled childhood was David Lewis Rice, who on Christmas Eve, 1985, murdered Seattle attorney Charles Goldmark, his wife, and two sons because he believed that Goldmark was the "head Jew" and "top Commie" (Communist) of the

Northwest. In reality, Goldmark was a highly respected liberal Christian. Rice also believed a theory found in some far-right hate literature that there were Communist Chinese poised in Canada and North Koreans lined up in Mexico ready to attack the United States. Rice's extreme paranoia was perhaps the result of a difficult childhood. His family had never shown him any love, and an accident as a child had left him scarred and blind in one eye, the target of countless jokes by his classmates. A loner because of his rejection by both his family and his classmates, Rice lived inside his head where his fantasies of persecution by other people grew to terrifying proportions and led him to his heinous final act.

Not all hate criminals are victims like Rice and Withrow, and not all people who grow up in troubled families commit hate crimes. Withrow, in fact, turned his back on his former colleagues when he was convinced by his girlfriend that it was better to love than to hate. He told a reporter, "I started thinking about all the people I had hurt for no reason. . . . I thought, 'These are human beings I've affected—I have taken children's minds and they are going out and committing crimes.'"[4] When he quit working with Metzger, he told Metzger, "I just don't want to hate nobody no more."[5]

In August 1993, when the plot to blow up the American Methodist Episcopal Church in Los Angeles (the largest, most influential African-American church in that city) was revealed, friends and neighbors of Christopher David Fisher, a twenty-year-old former Eagle Scout, were shocked to learn that he had confessed to his leadership in the plot. Fisher had grown up in a stable, upper-middle-class home. His mother was a college professor and his father an elementary school teacher. As an Eagle Scout, Fisher led a model life, encouraging other boys not to smoke or drink and to participate in recycling and other environmental activities. Unlike Withrow, he had not grown up in a house where racist language was common. But Fisher had joined the Fourth Reich Skinheads, an avowed hate group, and had quickly risen to a position of leadership within the group.

George Jones, the Maryland student guilty of killing a gay man, is currently serving time in prison for his action. Like Fisher, he was described by his teachers and neighbors as a "'good kid' from a 'good family.'"[6] He belonged to no organized hate group, and he and his friends attacked their victim just for fun. A reporter who visited the high school that Jones attended before the crime found only a few students who overtly supported Jones's decision to beat up a man just because he was gay. On the other hand, the reporter found "a walk through the school's halls, gym, and cafeteria reveals that many students make jokes about homosexuals, spread rumors about fellow students being gay, and frequently use the word 'faggot,' a disparaging term for gay men."[7]

To many observers, an atmosphere such as the one described at Jones's high school is the major reason for hate crimes and the growth of hate groups. The young white males who are committing these crimes are not operating in a vacuum. They are choosing targets based upon what they have heard at home or in the media. These crimes are no longer viewed as isolated actions. In all societies, teenage boys have always tended to be both violent and rebellious, more so than any other age group.

But it is only recently in the United States that this group has chosen in such large numbers to express their violence or rebellion in hate crimes.

Recently, David Dinkins, who was then mayor of New York, asked the question, "Who taught our children to hate so thoroughly and so mercilessly?"[8] The answer may be, "Everyone." Researchers have found that most babies by the age of two identify other babies according to sex and race. By the age of four or five, children use sex or race as reasons for not playing with other children. From this early age, "American culture spoonfeeds its children white cartoon characters, white angels, and good guys in white hats. These subtle but powerful cues teach children what sociologist Abraham Citron calls 'the rightness of whiteness . . .'"[9]

During their teenage years, all children wrestle with questions of identity as they grow into adults. For those who are prone to prejudice, it can be a source of self-esteem to put down—either verbally or physically—other people because of race, ethnic background, or sexual orientation, anything that makes their identity different from that of the attacker.

For those youngsters who tend toward violence, there are plenty of models for their actions. Although no one is yet absolutely sure about the impact of television on children, it is indisputable that American children watch a lot of television. By the age of sixteen, the average child may have watched 200,000 hours of television and has seen 200,000 acts of violence, including 50,000 murders.

There is one final explanation for why young men join hate groups—pure thrill. One observer of the rise of

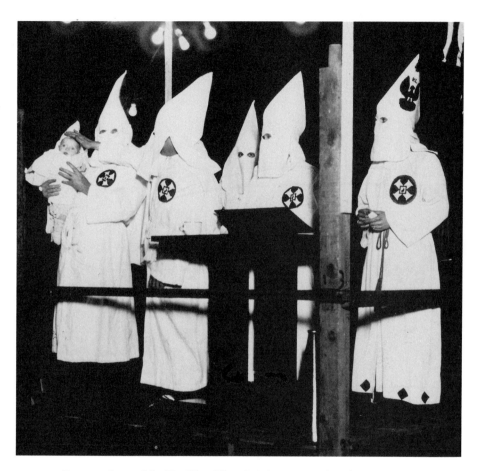

For members of the Ku Klux Klan, it is important that their message of hatred be carried to young people. The initiation of children and babies is an important part of Klan activities.

skinhead gangs in Germany has concluded that their growth has not resulted from the merger of the two halves of Germany, as unsettling as that has been, nor from poverty nor unemployment nor liberal permissiveness nor the breakdown of the family. Rather, he concludes that the young men in skinhead groups are "murderous punks" whose reward for terrorist acts is "not prison, but breathless TV coverage."[10] Other observers of Germany agree that the new skinheads are not the political storm troopers of Hitler's day who had a specific political agenda behind their hatred. Writes Jane Kramer:

> The skins say 'Heil Hitler!' but they know nothing about Hitler, or the war, beyond the fact that Hitler exterminated people who were 'different,' which is what they like to do themselves. They do not even know about the 'ethnic cleansing' going on a few hundred miles away in Bosnia now. They do not read newspapers. They read killer comic books and listen to Oi music, which is a kind of heavy-metal rock about the pleasures of genocide. . . . They do not know that other people think of Oi as a Yiddish word. They do not know Jews or anything about Jews, but Jews are certainly on their hit list, along with Turks, refugees and asylum seekers, anybody 'foreign.' . . . Most of them are not capable of—or interested in— explaining why they find foreign people or homeless people or handicapped people or any of the other people they kill unpleasant, or why they seem to enjoy killing those people. . . . They like to think of themselves as independent . . .[11]

"Independent" is one of the adjectives that was often

68

used to describe Robert Mathews, the leader of the Order. A reporter analyzing Mathews found that he, like the German skinheads, was an independent, uncomplicated, straightforward young man who was part of the American tradition of the frontier—"that part that regards a man as a law unto himself."[12] Mathews in another time might have been a swashbuckling pirate or a deerskin-clothed frontiersman, slaying enemies, but earning heroic praise instead of condemnation for killing Indians, for example. Disgruntled at the government over the issue of income taxes, Mathews moved to the farthest corner of Idaho. In the 1980s, however, Idaho was not the frontier that it was in the 1880s. In those days, Mathews could have escaped to an unpopulated frontier area and lived freely beyond the arm of the law, murdering at will anyone who trespassed on his property. In modern America, the popularity of Rambo reveals the depth of our respect for heroes who take the law into their own hands, deciding who shall live and who shall die. In real life, this kind of thinking can lead to hate crimes.

Whether hate crimes are committed by youths or older people, prejudice is at the root of the actions. Prejudice has been part of American society from the very beginning of colonial settlement. It continues and is most pervasive in neighborhoods where there is little contact with people who are different. When Yusuf Hawkins, a young African-American man, entered the community of Bensonhurst, New York, to look at a car that he had seen advertised, he was, for all intents and purposes, entering an alien territory. The vast majority of the people of Bensonhurst were white. The young men who attacked and killed Hawkins did not know many black people personally, and they were only too willing to assign racial stereotypes to the African-American stranger who suddenly appeared in their midst. They decided that he was there to date a white girl. It has long been part of the prejudicial myths about black men that they are a threat to white women. Without thinking through the validity of this stereotype, certainly without asking Hawkins, the white teens simply acted violently, shooting the young man, killing him and ruining their own lives.

Myth and paranoia about nonwhite Americans is particularly strong in rural areas of the United States, particularly in the West and Midwest. So it comes as no surprise that hate groups flourish in these areas. The people in these rural areas do not see many African Americans, Hispanics, Jews, or Asian Americans, and most of their neighbors or relatives who are gay keep that fact well-hidden or move away to urban areas where they can live more openly.

On October 23, 1984, Arthur Kirk, a Nebraska farmer, was killed in a shoot-out with a SWAT team of Nebraska state troopers. Kirk was bankrupt after a series of bad harvests, and as he brandished his M-16 in a futile attempt to keep his farm from being taken over by the bank, he thought that the troopers were agents of Mossad, the Israeli Secret Service. The anti-Semitism reflected in Kirk's dying actions is perhaps the most deeply rooted of the hatreds felt by white Americans in the rural Midwest and West.

Anti-Semitism is interwoven with the myth that the economy of the United States is controlled by international Jewish bankers. This myth is mentioned most often when times are bad in farm country, and since the mid-1970s times have been rough for American farmers. In a 1986 Harris poll taken in Nebraska and Iowa, the heart of farm country, nearly one-third of the people polled agreed with the statement, "Farmers have always been exploited by international Jewish bankers who are behind those who overcharge them for farm equipment or jack up the interest on their loans."[13] Nearly half of the population in both states agreed with the statement, "When it comes to choosing between people and money, Jews will choose money."[14] Even more damaging may be what James Coates calls "unexamined bigotry."[15] This is the casual use of hurtful, stereotypic language such as "jew down" (meaning "to drive a hard bargain") or "nigger in the woodpile" (meaning "to smell a rat"). The existence of this kind of unthinking prejudice among people who would never dream of committing a hate crime, argues Coates, "gives the haters a ready toehold."[16]

As devastating as the last decade has been for American farmers, they are not the only group to have suffered economically during this period of time. During the 1980s, the lower class in the United States grew larger and poorer. In 1977, 1 percent of the population controlled 7 percent of the nation's income; by 1990 this same small group controlled 11 percent of the nation's income. The number of millionaires doubled. During the same time, the percentage of children living in poverty increased from fewer than 15 percent to 20 percent. For the first time, Americans in the lower and middle classes believed that their children were not likely to have a better life than theirs. As they saw their share of the economic pie shrinking, it was inevitable that these people would look for villains to explain why this was happening to them. Under these circumstances, people turn to the stereotypic enemies that they have been taught are different and by their very differences are suspect of evil doing.

Fortunately, most people in these circumstances simply grumble and call names at the people they see on television. They may vote for right-wing politicians who promise to return America to its "rightful" owners, by which they mean white owners. David Duke, for example, attracted voters in 1986 when he proclaimed, "An America ruled by a majority of blacks, Mexicans and other Third World types will not be the America of our forefathers, or the kind of nation for which they struggled and sacrificed."[17] Without blatant racism, Duke made it clear that true Americans were not African American or Hispanic or Asian, and that true Americans were the ones who worked hard and sacrificed, and whose country was being threatened by those who are different.

When the city council of Dubuque, Iowa, came up with a plan that would offer incentives for African Americans to move to that small midwestern city, their goal was to diversify the population by increasing the number of black citizens from slightly over 1 percent to about 2 percent (far smaller than the national average). Then a recession hit, and Dubuque's citizens feared for their jobs. Their reaction against the tiny minority of newcomers was irrational but typical of the prejudiced thinking that can lead to hate crimes. Said one denizen of Dubuque, "Seems like they're getting everything and we're getting trounced on,"[18] even though the new African-American residents were just as vulnerable to the recession as older city inhabitants.

Most of Duke's followers and most of the residents of Dubuque, in fact most Americans who harbor prejudices against one group or another, are nonviolent. However, those who are violent hear the same messages. They learn "their culture and, as a result, [know] precisely those groups against which [they are] supposed to vent [their] anger."[19] In these few, however, tough economic times encourage violent reactions. When Vincent Chin was beaten to death in Detroit, his attackers made it clear that they blamed Chin—and other Asians—for the poor state of the American automobile industry. As they beat him, Ronald Ebens and Michael Nitz cried, "It's because of you we're out of work."[20]

Economic decline increases people's awareness of groups that they believe are competing with them for jobs and money. Increased visibility of minority groups can happen in other ways; it almost always leads to increased numbers of crimes targeted against members of the groups. For example, the number of attacks on gays and lesbians has increased with their increased visibility in society. Dr. Howard Ehrlich, research director of a national institute that monitors prejudice and violence, has noted, "When a traditionally subordinate group becomes more visible, levels of conflict increase."[21] Nearly invisible to the majority of Americans prior to the 1970s, since the revolution at the Stonewall Inn, gay Americans have become increasingly vocal about seeking equal civil rights with heterosexual Americans.

Gay and lesbian Americans have become more visible as they have adopted the tactics of other groups in working for greater civil rights.

Other groups also suffer from surges in criminal attack when they are featured on the front pages. Holocaust services on college campuses are often followed by increased anti-Semitic graffiti, such as swastikas painted on the walls of Jewish student centers. The Persian Gulf War heightened Americans' awareness of the Arab population living in the United States and consequently led to attacks on them and their property. When American car dealers in Detroit sponsored a series of advertisements implying that the Japanese were responsible for the decline in American car sales, Japanese Americans who had nothing to do with Japan or the car industry found themselves under attack. In one of the most violent incidents, a Japanese-American realtor in California was killed.

Whatever their motives, whatever their feelings, people who hate lose their right to speak out against other people because of their different skin color or religion or ethnic background when their prejudice turns violent. Criminal acts—trespass, vandalism, robbery, murder—are no less criminal because they are motivated by prejudice. In fact, in recent years, more and more people have come to believe that criminal actions are even more criminal when they are motivated by prejudice.

5

Does Freedom of Speech Mean Freedom to Hate?

As hate crimes have risen in number during the past five years, many state and city governments have attempted to deter, or prevent, such crimes by passing laws called bias laws. These laws make a crime that is motivated by hatred based on the victim's race, religion, ethnic background, or sexual orientation a more serious crime than such an act would ordinarily be. For example, if a person burns down a store because the owner of the store is an Arab, the crime is considered to be more serious than if the criminal simply burned down the store as a random act of vandalism. The criminal who commits a bias crime has to pay a larger price for his crime—either a stiffer fine or a longer jail sentence.

Many people believe that bias crime laws are unconstitutional. They believe that these laws violate the criminal's freedom of speech. If a person shouts "Kill the

Jew" as he shoots at a Jewish person, should he pay a higher penalty than a person who shouts, "Kill that guy?" People who are committed to freedom of speech believe that laws making the person shouting the epithet pay a higher price come perilously close to penalizing people for their thoughts. Suppose the second person hated Jews and was thinking that as he shot. Should his thoughts, if he reveals them in the courtroom, be the subject of higher penalties? The United States has always been committed to freedom of thought and speech. The concern is that bias laws move us down the road in the direction of those countries like Hitler's Germany that attempted to control how people thought about other people.

In the early 1980s, the Anti-Defamation League (A.D.L.) began to record a sharp increase in anti-Semitic incidents and crimes. At that point, the A.D.L. proposed a law that could be adopted by the individual states. The bias law drawn up by the A.D.L. had two primary components. First, the law included an institutional-vandalism measure that was particularly important in the case of crimes against Jews. This part of the law "prohibited and provided increased penalties for vandalizing, defacing or damaging places of worship, cemeteries, schools or community centers."[1] The second section of the law was called the intimidation statute. Under this provision, there would be enhanced penalties (stiffer sentences) for crimes like harassment or assault if they were committed because of the victim's race, color, religion, national origin, or sexual orientation.

Over the course of the 1980s all the states except Nebraska, Utah, and Wyoming adopted some form of hate crime statute. Institutional-vandalism laws were the most commonly accepted, but twenty-nine states also had bias-motivated violence and intimidation laws. Some states, such as New Jersey, had enhancement laws. If a crime was bias-related, the criminal's punishment was moved up one degree. For example, a person found guilty of murder in the third degree faced the harsher penalty of second-degree murder if the crime could be proved to be bias motivated. Sixteen states had laws making it illegal to burn crosses and fourteen to wear hoods, laws clearly aimed at the KKK.

In 1990, the federal government passed the Hate Crime Statistics Act. Although this is not bias-crime legislation in the strict sense that the state laws are, the act is proof that the federal government as well as the state governments recognized the special nature of hate crimes. Many observers were surprised when President George Bush, a conservative Republican, signed this bill into law. The statute had been held up in Congress for many years by other conservative politicians, especially Senator Jesse Helms of North Carolina, who objected to the inclusion of sexual orientation in the law. Many conservatives, like Helms, believe that homosexuality should in no way be condoned. He and his supporters believed that including antigay crimes with other hate crimes legitimized homosexuality as a way of life.

The law that President Bush signed simply requires the attorney general to keep statistical records on hate crimes. It does not in any way change the way that hate crimes are prosecuted on a federal level. In approving the law, Mr. Bush explained its purpose: "The faster we can find out about these hideous crimes, the faster we can track down the bigots who commit them."[2] As positive as Bush was about the law, it was not without its opponents. Helms's concerns were not the only ones that were voiced. Collecting the information may be difficult and is likely to be expensive. As terrible as hate crimes are, they make up a very small percentage of all crime in the United States. With drug-related crime escalating, many law enforcement officials would rather concentrate on crimes that they believe hurt a greater number of people.

Meanwhile, the state bias laws have come under attack from both the state and federal courts. Courts are the place where the constitutionality of laws is tested, and it has been in the courts that bias laws have come up against the First Amendment to the Constitution, which forbids laws that "abridge freedom of speech."

Late one night in June 1990, seventeen-year-old Robert Viktora, a white skinhead, snuck onto the yard of the only black family in a working-class neighborhood in St. Paul, Minnesota. Russ and Laura Jones were awakened by the flames that rose from the burning cross that Viktora planted on their yard. The youth had purposely chosen the traditional Ku Klux Klan symbol used to threaten violence against African Americans.

The local police could have charged Viktora with trespass or disturbing the peace, but they chose instead to charge him under the hate crime law that both the city of St. Paul and state of Minnesota had passed in the early 1980s. The city law made it illegal to place "on public or private property a symbol, object, appellation, characterization, or graffiti, including but not limited to, a burning cross or Nazi swastika, which one knows or

President George Bush signed into law the first Hate Crimes Statistics Act, a statute that required local law enforcement agencies to keep track of those crimes that seemed to be motivated by hate or bias.

has reasonable grounds to know arouses anger, alarm, or resentment in others on the basis of race, color, creed, or religion or gender."[3] Burning a cross on someone's lawn clearly fell under the prohibitions of this law.

What Viktora's lawyers and other defenders said in response was that the law itself was unconstitutional. They argued that the language of the law was so broad that it interfered with the right to free speech. At his first trial, the judge agreed that Viktora was guilty of trespass and damage to another's property, but he also agreed with the defense attorneys that the hate crime law was unconstitutional. The case then went to the Minnesota Supreme Court.

The supreme court disagreed with the first judge. According to the high court of Minnesota, Viktora's action was not protected by the First Amendment to the U.S. Constitution because the burning cross fell under the definition of "fighting words," which the United States Supreme Court in the case of *Chaplinsky* v. *New Hampshire* defined as "a direct tendency to cause acts of violence by the person to whom, individually, the remark is addressed."[4] Many defenders of the First Amendment, including organizations like the American Civil Liberties Union, which has a long history of fighting against racial and religious injustice, were not persuaded by the Supreme Court's arguments. As long as the "fighting words" statutes were on the books, they reasoned, there was no reason to have separate laws singling out specific ideas as being illegal.

Those who opposed the law pushed to take it before the United States Supreme Court, and on June 10, 1991, the Supreme Court agreed to hear the case, which was called *R.A.V. v. St. Paul.* (Viktora's initials were used because he was a juvenile at the time of the crime.)

A year later the Supreme Court rendered its decision against the St. Paul law. What the Supreme Court decided was similar to the decision of the first judge—they agreed with him that the law was too broad. By specifically mentioning certain forms of expression—the swastika or burning cross, for instance—the law, according to the Supreme Court, violated the free speech provisions of the First Amendment. Speaking for the majority of the justices on the Supreme Court, Justice Antonin Scalia argued that any law that limited forms of expression—such as the fighting words laws—had to be free of "content discrimination."[5] Many liberal-thinking people who do not usually agree with the conservative views of Justice Scalia agreed with him on this point. They argued that by singling out specific hateful words—for example, "nigger" or "fag" or "kike"—to be repressed, these words take on greater importance than they should. They also worried that content-based laws like the one in St. Paul could be expanded to "punish legitimate statements that upset people."[6]

In 1978 the U.S. Supreme Court had ruled in the case of *Village of Skokie* v. *National Socialist Party of America* that language or expression of ideas that offends or upsets people is protected under the First Amendment. In that case, the Supreme Court declared that the Nazis had the right to march down the street in a predominantly Jewish suburb. Clearly, the line between freedom of speech and "fighting words" is a fine one. Laura Jones, on whose lawn the cross was burned, said of Viktora, "He has the right to say anything he wants to, but he doesn't have a right to come up on our property and threaten us."[7]

Shortly after the Supreme Court's ruling on the Minnesota Viktora case, the Wisconsin Supreme Court struck down that state's hate crimes law. Once again the case was elevated to the United States Supreme Court. This time, however, the high court upheld the state law.

Wisconsin v. *Mitchell,* as the case was called when it was tried in front of the Supreme Court, began one night in October in Kenosha, Wisconsin. After seeing the movie "Mississippi Burning," which was about the early years of the civil rights movement, Todd Mitchell, a young black man, encouraged a group of his friends to "move on some white people."[8] Gregory Riddick, a fourteen-year-old white boy, had the misfortune to happen by at that moment. Mitchell cried to his friends, "There's a white boy. Go get him."[9] The boys beat Riddick until he was unconscious, causing brain damage that may well be with him for the rest of his life.

Todd Mitchell was sentenced to two years in prison for the beating. In addition, he was sentenced to two more years under the terms of the Wisconsin law that called for sentence enhancement (that is, greater penalties) in the case of crimes where criminals "intentionally select"[10] their victims because of religion, race, ethnic origin, disability, or sexual orientation. It was the additional two years that Mitchell's attorneys protested. As in the Minnesota case, they argued that the hate crimes law was unconstitutional. The U.S. Supreme Court, however, disagreed. Because the Wisconsin law targeted hate in general and did not refer specifically to any group, the Supreme Court found it constitutional. As Clarence

83

Thomas, the only African-American Supreme Court justice noted, the law could be used to try a group of black people who attacked another group of black people because they did not like their stand on civil rights.

Some people were concerned that the reason the Supreme Court upheld this law was that Mitchell was black. Since the vast majority of hate crimes are committed by the majority, that is white Americans, against members of minority groups, the Mitchell case was unusual. Those who are concerned about minority rights worried that this law could be used indiscriminately to increase the sentences of young black men committing crimes against victims who just happened to be white.

Other state laws will undoubtedly be tested, both by state courts and possibly by the Supreme Court. Ohio has already overturned its hate law; the court justified its action by saying that the law created "thought crime."[11] The case in question in Ohio arose from an incident at a campsite when a white man, angry at a black camper's loud music, threatened him, using racial epithets. What would have been a misdemeanor was escalated to a crime carrying the punishment of an eighteen-month jail sentence under the provisions of Ohio's hate law. No violent action, other than shouting, had taken place, however, and the judge in the case ruled that the Ohio law punished the white man's thinking and was in direct conflict with his freedom of speech.

A young man in Florida, Bradley Mills, is attempting to get his sentence overturned on the grounds that Florida's law is unconstitutional. He has been sentenced to fifty years in prison, more than twice as long as most similar offenders, for taking part in the murder of a

Vietnamese American who was beaten to death by a group of students who were yelling anti-Asian slogans as they killed him.

Proponents of hate crime laws, worried that state statutes will be struck down, are pushing for a federal hate crimes bill. Representative Charles E. Schumer of New York is the author of a bill that would direct the United States Sentencing Commission, the government agency responsible for setting the length of jail terms for federal crimes, to increase by three levels the sentence for anyone who is convicted of a crime that is "motivated by hatred, bias or prejudice, based on the [victim's] actual or perceived race, color, religion, national origin, ethnicity, gender or sexual orientation."[12] Although the bill passed the House of Representatives, it was tabled in the Senate, largely through the efforts of North Carolina's senior senator, Jesse Helms, who was again concerned that this bill, like the Hate Crimes Statistics Act, might be construed as condoning homosexuality.

Other people oppose the bill on the same grounds that they have opposed similar state bills. They argue that the federal law would be unconstitutional because it makes some people's lives more valuable than others. As one critic wrote in opposition to the Washington, D.C., Bias-Related Crime Act of 1989, "The legislation in effect divides America into two classes: Those whose skulls can be cracked with a criminal penalty of, let us say, six months in jail, and those whose skulls are better protected by government and thus warrant nine months in jail if cracked."[13]

The inclusion of gender in the Schumer bill raises another interesting and controversial aspect of hate crime legislation. Should attacks on women, particularly rape, count as hate crimes?

Is all rape, by its very nature, an attack based on gender? Several United States senators apparently think so. Under the leadership of Senator Joseph Biden, its chief sponsor, the Violence Against Women Act, if passed, would enhance penalties for violent crimes that are "motivated by gender."[14] This law, had it been in effect at the time of the infamous "Central Park jogger" case, would have doubled or tripled the sentences of the young men who brutally attacked and raped the jogger. The "Central Park jogger" was a young woman who was jogging near her apartment in New York City when she was assaulted and raped by several young men who left her for dead. Although she did not die, she will bear the lifelong scars from the incident, both physical and mental. Although the attackers were black and the victim was white, it appeared that they were motivated more by her gender than her race, and the crime was not treated as a bias attack.

Once again, the bill's opponents are concerned that it violates the First Amendment because again courts will be asked to judge what a person was thinking at the time of a crime. Some feminists are concerned because there may develop a distinction between a bad rape and a worse one (one motivated by hatred), and feminists have worked hard during the past decade to educate people about the horrors of all rapes, whether committed by a stranger in the night or a date on a college campus.

Whatever the outcome of the Schumer bill or the Biden bill, one thing is clear. In the wake of increased violence based on hatred, the United States has turned to

Conservative thinkers such as Phyllis Schlafly (center) argue that women should not work outside the home. They argue that the rightful order of society is threatened by increasing civil rights for minority groups.

the law to help end the hostility and crime. There is always a danger in repressing the rights of criminals. That danger is that the rights of all people will be abridged. In a democracy, the majority must safeguard the rights of minorities. At times that means protection from criminal actions, but it also means protection for unpopular views. In the case of hate crime legislation, these two goals sometimes conflict.

6

Teenagers and Hate Groups

Hate groups can only flourish if they continue to recruit new members. From the increase in violence at high schools and on college campuses, it looks as though they are having no trouble finding young people who are willing to join in hating other people because they are different. Many people think that the reason young people are willing to join hate groups in high school and in college is that they are uncertain about their own futures. Because they believe that the American economic pie is shrinking, they are worried that other people will get a bigger slice. White males, especially, believe that blacks, Hispanics, women, and Asians should not take pieces of a pie that belong to them.

In 1990 a poll was taken among high school students that found that 21 percent of them had witnessed racial or religious hate incidents "very often" and another 36 percent witnessed such incidents "once in a while."[1] Over all, then, more than half the teens surveyed had witnessed some form of hate incident. Between 1986 and 1990, New York City law enforcement officials recorded an 80 percent increase in hate crimes, and 70 percent of those crimes were committed by people under 19.

Often people believe that the young people who join hate groups are those with the least education and the least to hope for in the future in the way of jobs. As a Berkeley, California sociologist has put it, "We used to assume that prejudice would go away when a more enlightened, higher-educated group of young people replaced a generation of bigots. That doesn't follow any more."[2] Increasingly, hate has flourished on college campuses.

Consider these incidents, for example. In the fall of 1990, students at the University of Illinois surrounded a Jewish fraternity and shouted, "Hitler had the right idea."[3] At Brown University in Providence, Rhode Island, the campus was littered with anonymous pamphlets that read, "Once upon a time Brown was a place where a white man could go to class without having to look at little black faces, or little yellow faces, or little brown faces, except when he went to take his meals. Things have been going downhill since the kitchen help moved into the classroom. Keep white supremacy alive."[4] At the University of Alaska, students sported T-shirts advertising their membership in the "Anti-fag Society," and at Syracuse University, students with similar ideas wore t-shirts advocating violence against homosexuals—"Club faggots, not seals." At Rutgers University and at the University of Wisconsin,

90

students vandalized campus Jewish student centers and at Yale University, the Afro-American Cultural Center was damaged.

On hundreds of college campuses in the 1980s, the response to the increase in racial and religious incidents was the development of campus speech codes. At Brown, at Wisconsin, at Michigan, at Stanford, policies were instituted that punished students for using language that targeted other people because of race, religion, national origin, or sexual orientation. Many people, however, felt that these codes of conduct infringed on students' freedom of speech.

One controversial incident involved a student at Brown University who stood in the middle of the campus and yelled nasty epithets about blacks, gays, and Jews. He was expelled. The president of Brown claimed that the student had been expelled for his raucous behavior, but many people believed that if he had been just as raucous and had been yelling football cheers, he would have been laughed at and certainly not expelled. It appeared as though he had been denied his right to freedom of speech.

A student who was expelled from the University of Michigan for using violent language appealed his case to a federal court. The Michigan speech code prohibited "discriminatory comments, epithets and abusive language [based on] race, sex, religion, sexual orientation, national origin or age."[5] The federal court agreed with the student and found the Michigan speech code to be unconstitutional in 1991.

Although the legal system often provides a way for victims of hate crimes to defend themselves against their attackers, nothing protects the victims of hate crimes from the hurt and pain that bias crime brings—even when the crime is limited to hateful words. A Jewish girl who heard anti-Semitic remarks whispered about her in the hallway of her high school has said that she will never forget how bad she felt when she heard the hateful words directed at her because of her religion.[6] Her experience was not very different from that of 18-year-old Gordon Diefenbach, a gay teenager who eventually quit attending his Denver, Colorado, high school because of the physical and verbal attacks against him because of his homosexuality. Gordon remembers high school as a time of isolation: "If a teacher would have the class split up into groups, no one would want to be in my group. . . . Two years ago I tried to kill myself. I slit my wrists. . . . I didn't think I could go through life with everyone beating up on me, harassing me, hating me."[7] Gordon Diefenbach's experience was the same as that of any minority group that finds itself victimized. No matter how secure a person is, the sense of isolation, coupled with overt or implied violence because of the person's difference, is often more than a person can stand.

Being singled out for one's differences can be particularly painful during adolescence. In February 1994, a young woman named Revonda Bowen sat in an assembly at her high school in Wedowee, Alabama, and heard the principal announce that no black girls or boys could attend the prom with white boys or girls. She stood up and bravely asked the principal what she should do about the prom since her mother is black and her father is white. The principal replied that her mother and father had "made a mistake, having a mixed-race child."[8]

By expressing his belief that certain types of people are "mistakes," her principal was isolating Revonda from her classmates. The pain and embarrassment Revonda felt caused her to burst into tears. Shortly after the incident, the school board voted to suspend the principal, and Morris Dees of the Southern Poverty Law Center has volunteered to prosecute Hulond Humphries, the principal, on Revonda's behalf. No matter what the outcome of the case, however, Revonda will never be able to forget that moment in front of her entire high school when a person in authority said that she should never have been born because she was an example of "race-mixing." Furthermore, there is no guarantee that Mr. Humphries will be found guilty of any crime.

Prohibiting hatred by limiting what people may say about other people appears to be unconstitutional. So how should people who want to end hatred and violence go about it? The best way is more education. At several high schools in the New York City area, a program dedicated to the memory of Yusuf Hawkins asks teenagers to talk openly about their prejudices. They are allowed to use the words that have been outlawed on some college campuses, but they must do so openly in a classroom where classmates who are black or Jewish or gay can hear them. Although the initial reaction is one of hurt and shock, by talking about their feelings and stereotypes, they reach a better understanding of one another. In a truly democratic society, schools have a moral obligation to uphold freedom of speech. The best way to end hate speech is by showing with better words how harmful hatred can be.

Other school programs that are helping educate

teenagers about the connections between hatred and violence are "A World of Difference," sponsored by the Anti-Defamation League, and "The Tolerance Project" sponsored by Barbara Jordan, the former congresswoman from Texas. Both programs have received national support from teachers' associations and school boards. Neither program shies away from the language of hate; instead, they help students examine the motivations behind such talk.

There are many organizations in the United States today that are committed to democracy and free speech and to ending hatred and violence. For more information, you can write to these groups, which are listed in "Further Information." By discussing openly and honestly why we fear those who are different, we can stop hatred. When someone says something hateful about another person, it is not enough to say, "Shut up." We need to ask why that person feels that way. When we listen to song lyrics or comedian's jokes that use put-downs of other people, we need to ask why, and we need to consider whether we want to repeat those jokes and buy those records. Everyone thinking and working together can reverse the hatred in American society.

Further Information

Groups that are concerned about hatred and hate groups in American society include the following:

Anti-Defamation League
823 United Nations Plaza
New York, NY 10017

Center for Democratic Renewal
P.O. Box 50469
Atlanta, GA 30302

National Gay and Lesbian Task Force
1517 U St., NW
Washington, DC 20009

Southern Poverty Law Center
400 Washington Ave.
Montgomery, AL 36104

Two programs that can be used in schools to teach about tolerance are:

"A World of Difference"
Anti-Defamation League
823 United Nations Plaza
New York, NY 10017

"Teaching Tolerance"
Southern Poverty Law Center
400 Washington Ave.
Montgomery, AL 36104

Notes by Chapter

Chapter 1

1. Jack Levin and Jack McDevitt, *Hate Crimes: The Rising Tide of Bigotry and Bloodshed* (New York: Plenum Press, 1993), p. 8.

2. Katie Monagle, "Portrait of Hate Crime," *Scholastic Update* (April 3, 1992), p. 5.

3. "Counting Hate Crimes Proves to be Difficult Task," *CQ Researcher* (January 8, 1993), p. 6.

4. Levin and McDevitt, p. 33.

Chapter 2

1. H. Rap Brown, press conference in Chicago, 1967.

2. Michael and Judy Ann Newton, *Racial and Religious Violence in America: A Chronology* (New York: Garland Publishers, 1991), p. ix.

3. Ibid.

4. James Coates, *Armed and Dangerous: The Rise of the Survivalist Right* (New York: Hill and Wang, 1987), p. 23.

5. Ibid. p. 33.

6. Jack Levin and Jack McDevitt, *Hate Crimes: The Rising Tide of Bigotry and Bloodshed* (New York: Plenum Press, 1993), p. 96.

7. Kenneth Jost, "Hate Crimes," *CQ Researcher* (January 8, 1993), p. 13.

Chapter 3

1. Claire Safran, "Our Life in the Ku Klux Klan," *Good Housekeeping* (June 1992), p. 139.

2. Lauren Tarshis, "Brotherhood of Bigots," *Scholastic Update* (April 3, 1992), p. 12.

3. Elinor Langer, "The American neo-Nazi Movement Today," *The Nation* (July 16/23, 1990), p. 95.

4. James Coates, *Armed and Dangerous: The Rise of the Survivalist Right* (New York: Hill and Wang, 1987).

5. Mark Starr, "Violence on the Right," *Newsweek* (March 4, 1985), p. 25.

6. Ibid. p. 23.

7. Ted Gest, "Sudden Rise of Hate Groups Spurs Federal Crackdown," *U.S. News and World Report* (May 6, 1985), p. 68.

8. Coates, p. 57.

9. Ibid. p. 58.

10. Ibid. p. 52.

11. Ibid. p. 104.

12. Tarshis, p. 2.

13. Jack Levin and Jack McDevitt, *Hate Crimes: The Rising Tide of Bigotry and Bloodshed* (New York: Plenum Press, 1993), p. 103.

14. Joseph Berger, "Forum for Bigotry? Fringe Groups on TV," *New York Times* (May 23, 1993), p. 34.

15. Langer, p. 85.

16. Ibid. p. 89.

17. "Fugitive Surrenders after Idaho Siege," *Facts on File* (September 17, 1992), p. 686.

Chapter 4

1. Morris Dees, "Young, Gullible and Taught to Hate," *New York Times* (August 25, 1993), p. 32.

2. Helen Zia, "Women in Hate Groups," *Ms.* (March/April, 1991).

3. Dees, p. 32.

4. Michelle Green, "Trouble," *People* (September 21, 1987), p. 45.

5. Ibid.

6. Katie Monagle, "Portrait of a Hate Crime," *Scholastic Update* (April 3, 1992), p. 5.

7. Ibid. p. 7.

8. Herbert Buchsbaum, "Why Do People Hate?" *Scholastic Update* (April 3, 1992), p. 9.

9. Ibid.

10. Josef Joffe, "Why 1992 is Different from 1932," *U.S. News and World Report* (December 14, 1992), p. 33.

11. Jane Kramer, "Neo-Nazis: A Chaos in the Head," *The New Yorker* (June 14, 1993), pp. 52–55.

12. L. J. Davis, "Ballad of an American Terrorist," *Harper's Magazine* (July 1986), p. 53.

13. James Coates, *Armed and Dangerous: The Rise of the Survivalist Right* (New York: Hill and Wang, 1987), p. 197.

14. Ibid. p. 198.

15. Ibid. p. 262.

16. Ibid.

17. Jack Levin and Jack McDevitt, *Hate Crimes: The Rising Tide of Bigotry and Bloodshed* (New York: Plenum Press, 1993), p. 37.

18. Ibid. p. 84.

19. Ibid. p. 48.

20. Ibid. p. 58.

21. George M. Anderson, "People Are Getting Hurt," *Commonwealth* (February 26, 1993), p. 16.

Chapter 5

1. Kenneth Jost, "Hate Crimes," *CQ Researcher* (January 8, 1993), p. 12.

2. Ibid. p. 14.

3. "Breaking the Codes," *The New Republic* (July 8, 1993), p. 12.

4. Jost, p. 14.

5. Ibid.

6. "Breaking the Codes," p. 8.

7. Ibid.

8. "Bad Motives," *The New Yorker* (June 21, 1993), p. 4.

9. Ibid.

10. Jeffrey Rosen, "Bad Thoughts," *The New Republic* (July 5, 1993), p. 15.

11. Jost, p. 15.

12. Ibid. p. 16.

13. John Leo, "The Politics of Hate," *U.S. News and World Report* (October 9, 1989), p. 24.

14. Ruth Shalit, "Caught in the Act," *The New Republic* (July 12, 1993), p. 12.

Chapter 6

1. "How Did You Respond?," *Scholastic Update* (April 3, 1992), p. 16.

2. Art Levine, "America's Youthful Bigots," *U.S. News and World Report* (May 7, 1990), p. 59.

3. Ibid.

4. Pete Hamill, "Black and White at Brown," *Esquire* (April 1990), pp. 67–68.

5. Kenneth Jost, "Hate Crimes," *CQ Researcher* (January 8, 1993), p. 18.

6. Lauren Tarshis, "The Ugly American," *Scholastic Update* (April 3, 1992), p. 2.

7. Lauren Tarshis, "The Voice of a Victim," *Scholastic Update* (April 3, 1992), p. 2.

8. Bob Herbert, "The Prom and the Principal," *New York Times* (March 16, 1994), p. A21.

Further Reading

Billington, Ray Allen. *The Protestant Crusade: A Study of the Origins of American Nativism.* New York: MacMillan, 1938.

Coates, James. *Armed and Dangerous: The Rise of the Survivalist Right.* New York: Hill and Wang, 1987.

Cook, Fred J. *The Ku Klux Klan: America's Recurring Nightmare.* New York: Messner, 1980.

Hacker, Andrew. *Two Nations: Black and White, Separate, Hostile, Unequal.* New York: MacMillan, 1992.

Levin, Jack and Jack McDevitt. *Hate Crimes: The Rising Tide of Bigotry and Bloodshed.* New York: Plenum Press, 1993.

Newton, Michael and Judy Ann. *Racial and Religious Violence In America: A Chronology.* New York: Garland Publishers, 1991.

Terkel, Studs. *Race: How Blacks and Whites Feel About the American Obsession.* New York: New Press, 1993.

Wade, Wyn Craig. *The Fiery Cross: The Ku Klux Klan in America.* New York: Simon and Schuster, 1987.

Index